# SOLVING SCIENCE MYSTERIES

# Why Do Balls Bounce?

## All About Gravity

**Rob Moore**

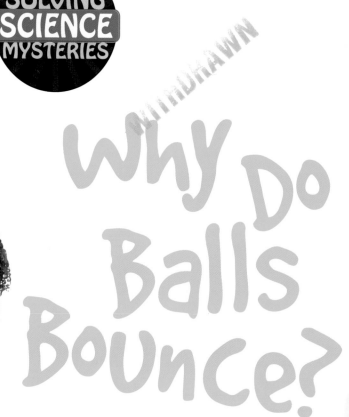

**PowerKiDS press**

New York

D1472847

Published in 2010 by The Rosen Publishing Group, Inc.
29 East 21st Street, New York, NY 10010

Copyright © 2010 Denise Ryan & Associates

All rights reserved. No part of this book may be reproduced in any format without permission in writing from the publisher, except by a reviewer.

Produced and designed by Denise Ryan & Associates
Editor: Helen Moore
Designer: Anita Adams
Photographer: Lyz Turner-Clark
U.S. Editor: Joanne Randolph

Photo Credits: p. 4: © Photographer: Lorna | Agency: Dreamstime.com; p. 5: Jaimie D. Travis; p. 6 top: DK Images; p. 6 and 7 bottom: Fotolibra; p. 7 top: Lynne Lancaster; pp. 8 and 13 top NASA; p. 10: Andrea Leone; p. 11 top: Brandon Laufenberg; p. 11 middle: Bob Smith; p. 11 third from top: Brandon Laufenberg; p. 12 top: Bob Cheung; p. 12 bottom: Adam Brouwer; pp. 13 top and 14 top: NASA; pp. 13 middle, 16 top and 17 top: Photolibrary; p. 13 bottom: Courtesy Kenneth Ford and the Metanexus Institute; p. 14 bottom: Jeff McDonald; p. 15 top: © Photographer: Jim Parkin | Agency: Dreamstime.com; p. 16 bottom: Elvis Santana; p. 17 bottom: Emiliano Spada; p. 18 bottom: David Lewis; p. 19 top: © Photographer: Drazen Vukelic | Agency: Dreamstime.com; p. 21: © Photographer: Erengoksel | Agency: Dreamstime.com; p. 22 left: © Photodisc; p. 22 right: Shutterstock.com.

Library of Congress Cataloging-in-Publication Data

Moore, Rob.
  Why do balls bounce? : all about gravity / Rob Moore.
    p. cm. — (Solving science mysteries)
  Includes index.
  ISBN 978-1-61531-889-6 (lib. bdg.) — ISBN 978-1-61531-910-7 (pbk.) —
ISBN 978-1-61531-911-4 (6-pack)
  1. Gravity—Juvenile literature. 2. Gravity—Miscellanea—Juvenile literature. 3. Mass (Physics)—
Juvenile literature. 4. Mass (Physics)—Miscellanea—Juvenile literature. I. Title.
  QC178.M664 2010
  531'.14—dc22
                          2009024988

Manufactured in the United States of America

CPSIA Compliance Information: Batch #WW10PK: For Further Information contact Rosen Publishing, New York, New York at 1-800-237-9932

# Contents

# Questions About Gravity

## Q: What is gravity?

A: Gravity is an invisible **force**. If you drop something, it falls toward your feet. This is because everything on Earth is held in place by gravity. Earth's gravity pulls everything down toward the ground—so without gravity we would all float up into the sky and our oceans would spill into space! Earth is not the only place in space where this force is at work—gravity exists everywhere in the universe.

# Q: Why don't skydivers fly off into space?

A: Skydivers don't fly off into space because the force of gravity pulls them toward Earth. When skydivers dive from an aircraft, their falling speed increases until their weight is balanced by the force of the air. This force, called **air resistance**, acts in the opposite direction to gravity. Once they have met this force, the skydivers continue to fall at a steady rate as Earth's gravity draws them down.

## Q: Does gravity keep the planets in place?

A: Yes, the Sun's gravity keeps the planets in place. The planets travel in a straight line past the Sun but, as they approach it, the Sun's gravity draws them toward it. This makes them travel in a curve. When the planets are closest to the Sun, its gravity flings them away, exactly like a stone being slung from a catapult. Eventually the Sun's gravity slows the planets enough to be able to draw them back, until the same action occurs again. This causes the planets to follow an **ellipse** in their orbit around the Sun.

*The Sun*

*Earth*

*The Moon*

*Earth follows an elliptical path around the Sun.*

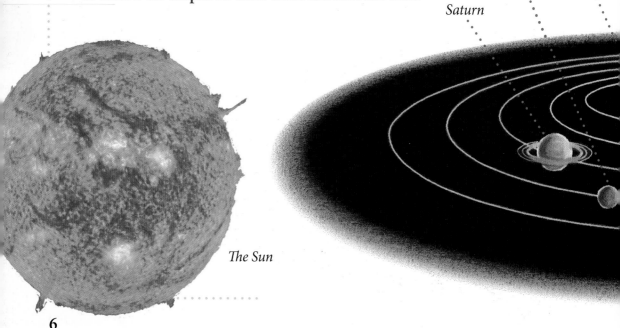

*Saturn*

*Uranus*

*Earth*

*The Sun*

*The Moon orbits Earth in an ellipse.*

## Q: Does gravity hold the Moon in place, too?

A: Yes, it does. Just as the pull of the Sun holds the planets in its orbit, Earth's gravity holds the Moon in its orbit. The Moon is also affected by the gravity of the Sun, but because the Moon is so much closer to Earth than it is to the Sun, the Moon appears to orbit only Earth. The distance between Earth and the Moon ranges from about 223,694 to 251,655 miles (360,000–405,000 km) depending upon the Moon's position in its orbit.

### Driving the Distance

The distance between Earth and the Moon when they are farthest apart is equivalent to driving from New York to Los Angeles about 102 times. If we drove that distance at 65 miles per hour (105 km/h), it would take us about 161 days to complete the journey. If we started on June 1, we would finish on November 8!

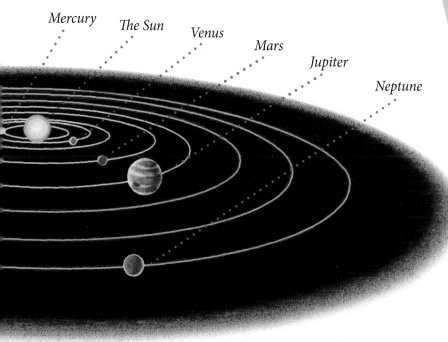

*Mercury*   *The Sun*   *Venus*   *Mars*   *Jupiter*   *Neptune*

# Questions About Mass and Weight

**Q:** What is the difference between mass and weight?

**A:** Mass is the amount of material in an object. It stays the same unless some material is removed. Weight is a combination of the force of gravity on the object and its mass. So weight can be different according to, say, the height above Earth or the depth below sea level.

**Q:** Are astronauts really weightless when they are orbiting Earth?

**A:** Astronauts in Earth's orbit are not weightless, but they feel like they are. The **sensations** they experience are the same as those that we feel when we are on some amusement park rides. Not only are the weightlessness sensations the same for astronauts and roller-coaster riders, but the causes are also the same. We feel like we are weightless when there are no external objects touching our bodies, exerting a push or pull upon them.

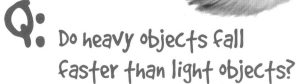

# Q: Do heavy objects fall faster than light objects?

A: All objects fall at the same rate at the same **altitude**. Some objects appear to fall faster or slower because of their air resistance and because they hit the ground with more force. A brick appears to fall faster than a feather, which "floats." It hits the ground with more force, too. Sir Isaac Newton showed that the force of a falling object is equal to its mass multiplied by its **acceleration.**

Acceleration due to gravity changes with altitude. At sea level it is 32.2 feet per second per second (9.82 m/s²), but at the Mount Everest base camp it is 32.1 feet per second per second (9.8 m/s²). On Mount Everest you would not only weigh less but you would not fall down as fast!

# Questions About Motion

## Q: How do fly balls fly?

**A:** Fly balls fly because of the force of the hit. That force drives them up away from Earth. But instead of flying off into space, the balls are pulled back down by Earth's gravity. The balls' flight is a **parabola** that ends when the balls land or are caught.

## Q: Why do balls bounce?

A: Balls bounce because a ball's fall produces a force against the ground, and because the Earth is so much bigger, the ball is dented. This dent produces another force that tries to get the ball back into shape. The force of the ball returning to its first shape is greater than the force of gravity, so it bounces away from Earth. Eventually Earth's gravity will cancel the ball's bounce and the ball will come down again. If you watch a game of tennis you can see these forces in action.

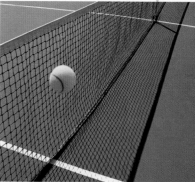

## Q: What does "momentum" mean?

A: Momentum means "mass in motion." All objects have mass; so if an object is moving, then it has momentum—it has its mass in motion. The amount of momentum an object has depends upon how much is moving and how fast it is going. A big truck is going to be harder to stop than a small truck, even if they are moving at the same speed.

# It's a Fact

### > Earth Moves, Too

If you fall over, gravity pulls you down but your body also pulls Earth up toward you! Because Earth is so much bigger than your body, its movement is very small and you don't notice it.

### > Tidal Bulge

The gravitational pull of the Moon creates tides on Earth. All the oceans are pulled by the Moon's gravity. The tidal bulge that occurs at high tide follows the revolution of the Moon. Earth rotates eastward through the bulge once every 24 hours and 50 minutes.

### > High Tides

When there is a high tide on one side of the planet, there is also a high tide on the planet's opposite side due to the **inertia** of the ocean. While Earth is being pulled toward the Moon by its gravitational field, the ocean on the opposite side is not, which creates a high tide on that side of the planet, too.

## > Black Holes

Cygnus X–1 was the first known object that was described as a **black hole**. It was discovered in 1970 and by 1972 was known to be a star system that was only a few miles (km) wide. One of the stars was so **dense** that it was considered to be a black hole.

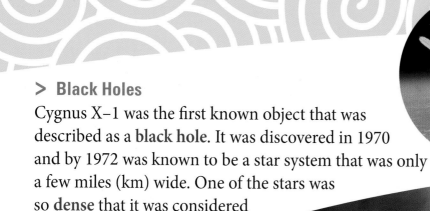

## Immense Gravity

The American scientist John Wheeler was the first person to use the term "black hole" in 1968. He used this term for star systems that appear black to observers. Any object falling into a black hole becomes dimmer and dimmer as the light from it is drawn in by the immense gravity.

*Dr. John Wheeler being presented with a book inspired by his work*

13

# Can You Believe It?

## Gravity Shrinks You!

Gravity actually makes us shorter! The spongy discs between the vertebrae of our spine **compress** under the effects of gravity. If we reduce the force of gravity on our spine by lying down, this material relaxes and we can be slightly taller than we were. Astronauts who were working in the Skylab missions had to have their space suits designed to take into account that they would be taller once they were free of Earth's gravity.

## Don't Fall!

If you jumped from an aircraft flying above Earth, after 5 seconds you would be falling at about 164 feet per second (50 m/s). That's 112 miles per hour (180 km/h)! If you jumped from an aircraft flying above Jupiter, you would be falling at twice that speed, 224 miles per hour (360 km/h). On Earth you would have fallen 1,640 feet (500 m), but on Jupiter you would have fallen about 13,123 feet (4,000 m). On either planet you would need a parachute!

## Which World?

In 1987 Stefka Kostadinova of Bulgaria established a new world record for the women's high jump. She jumped 6.85 feet (2.09 m). If Stefka had made this jump under the gravity of Mars, she would have jumped about 18 feet (5.5 m). On Jupiter she would have jumped less than 3.3 feet (1 m). Gravity on Mars is about a third that of Earth's and on Jupiter it is more than double.

## Escaping from Earth

Depending upon how fast a spacecraft travels, it may go into a circular, elliptical, or highly elliptical orbit around Earth. If it reaches a **velocity** of 24,979 miles per hour (40,200 km/h), the spacecraft escapes from Earth's gravity altogether.

Deep space probes use the pull of gravity from each planet they pass to change their course and speed on to the next planet. *Pioneer 10* flew past Jupiter while the flight path of the *Pioneer 11* probe took it past Jupiter and on to Saturn!

# Who Found out?

## Revolution: Galileo Galilei

Galileo Galilei (1564–1642) was an Italian scientist who studied the way objects fall by dropping them from the Leaning Tower of Pisa. He became famous when he was accused of **heresy** because he believed Earth revolved around the Sun. Galileo made great improvements to the design of telescopes and made many astronomical discoveries. He studied lunar craters and found and named the four moons of Jupiter. Sir Isaac Newton based some of his theories on Galileo's.

*The Leaning Tower of Pisa, Italy*

# Theories of Gravity: Isaac Newton

English-born Sir Isaac Newton (1643–1727) is considered to be one of the greatest mathematicians and **physicists** of all time. He started developing his famous theories of gravity when he saw an apple fall from a tree. Newton thought there must be a force acting on the apple because as it fell it travelled faster. He reasoned that the same force would still be acting if the tree were twice, or even ten times as tall. He thought that the force might be **universal** and if it was it would explain the way planets orbit the Sun, and the Moon orbits Earth.

# Physicist:
# Albert Einstein

Albert Einstein (1879–1955) was born in Germany. He is regarded as one of the greatest physicists to have ever lived. Einstein examined Isaac Newton's theory of gravity. He pointed out that a person would not be able to tell the difference between feeling gravity pulling them to Earth and being pulled down by an elevator that was traveling at a certain speed. Albert Einstein was awarded the Nobel Prize for Physics in 1921 and was named *Time* magazine's Man of the Century. His name is often used to describe someone who is very intelligent.

*Elevators ascending and descending on the side of a building*

## Skydiving: Joseph Kittinger

In 1960 U.S. Air Force captain Joseph Kittinger (1928– ) set the world record for the longest and fastest sky dive. He jumped from a helium balloon at 102,690 feet (31,330 m) and dived for 4 minutes and 36 seconds.

He released his parachute about 1,640 feet (5,000 m) from the ground, having fallen at speeds of up to 684 miles per hour (1,100 km/h). During the dive, he was the first person to travel faster than the speed of sound without an aircraft or a spacecraft.

# It's Quiz Time!

The pages where you can find the answers are shown in the red circles, except where otherwise noted.

## Unscramble the person's name.

1. i in teens    (18)

2. kitten rig    (19)

3. ail lego    (16)

4. now ten    (17)

## Find the odd one out. Answers on bottom of page 21.

| | | | |
|---|---|---|---|
| 1. mass | weight | gravity | speed |
| 2. Earth | black hole | Jupiter | Moon |
| 3. speed | velocity | volume | acceleration |
| 4. tide | sea level | ocean | altitude |

## Choose the correct words.

1. You would be heaviest under the gravity of (Jupiter, Mercury, Earth).    (15)

2. Mass (is, is not) the same as weight.    (8)

3. Objects fall (faster, slower) at higher altitudes.    (9)

4. A person would be (shorter, taller) on Earth than on Jupiter.    (15)

**Complete these sentences.**

1. Mass is the amount of _____ in an object.  ⑧

2. Planets orbit the Sun in an _____ .  ⑥

3. Einstein examined _____ _____ theory of gravity.  ⑱

4. All objects fall at the same speed at the same _____ .  ⑨

Answers: 1. speed  2. black hole  3. volume  4. altitude

# Try It Out!

Go back and read about whether heavy objects fall faster than light ones on page 9 again. Now get ready to put those ideas into action!

## What You'll Need:

- Some heavy and some light objects, such as a rock, ball, cotton ball, or paper clip
- Some flat, light objects, such as an index card, envelope, leaf, or feather

**1** First let's try out the idea that objects fall at the same rate from the same height. Hold your arms out in front of you, holding two of your objects from the first list above. Now let go! Which one lands first? (They should land at the same time.)

**2** Now try the same thing using one of the objects from the first group and one of the flat objects from the second group. Which one lands first this time? (The flat one likely landed last because of air resistance.)

# Glossary

**acceleration** (ik-SEH-luh-ray-shun) Increase in the rate or speed of something.

**air resistance** (EHR rih-ZIS-tens) The gases surrounding Earth opposing the force of gravity.

**altitude** (AL-tuh-tood) Height above sea level.

**black hole** (BLAK HOHL) A region in space where matter is so dense that anything approaching it will disappear.

**compress** (kum-PRES) Press or squeeze together.

**dense** (DENTS) Thick, closely packed.

**ellipse** (ih-LIPS) A stretched circle shape.

**force** (FORS) An influence that causes something to move. It may be a lift, a push, or a pull and it has a size and a direction.

**gravity** (GRA-vih-tee) The force of attraction between objects.

**heresy** (HER-eh-see) Any belief or teaching that opposes the established beliefs.

**inertia** (ih-NER-shuh) Inaction.

**mass** (MAS) The amount of matter contained in an object.

**parabola** (puh-RAH-buh-luh) The curved path of an object that is projected at an angle to Earth's surface.

**physicists** (FIH-zuh-sists) Scientists who study the natural laws and properties of matter and energy.

**sensations** (sen-SAY-shunz) Feelings or impressions that are not necessarily based on reality.

**universal** (YOO-neh-ver-sul) Including or affecting everything.

**velocity** (veh-LAH-seh-tee) The speed of a moving object.

**weight** (WAYT) The effect of gravity on a mass.

# Index

# Web Sites

Due to the changing nature of Internet links, PowerKids Press has developed an online list of Web sites related to the subject of this book. This site is updated regularly. Please use this link to access the list:

*www.powerkidslinks.com/ssm/bounce/*